THE
STORY
of GOD
with US

Written by
KENNETH PADGETT
& SHAY GREGORIE

Illustrated by
AEDAN PETERSON

Wolfbane
BOOKS

KENNETH PADGETT and his wife, Rebecca, live in the South Carolina Lowcountry with their two young daughters. Kenneth is a PhD (cand) in Biblical Studies at Trinity College, Bristol (UK) and serves in his local church as the Scholar-In-Residence. He also holds a Master's degree in Old Testament from Gordon-Conwell Theological Seminary. He's a lover of Narnian ships, heroic rabbits, and a big bowl of shrimp & grits!

SHAY GREGORIE is a native of Mount Pleasant, South Carolina where he lives with his wife, Catherine, and their eight children. He is an ordained pastor in the Anglican Church of North America and currently serves on the pastoral staff in his local church. He holds a Master of Divinity degree from Gordon-Conwell Theological Seminary. If he had to be a different creature, he'd be an Ent, maybe a marsh-wiggle, but he's mostly marsh-wiggle already.

AEDAN PETERSON is an illustrator and visual developer based in Nashville. He's been busy for the last few years, illustrating the new edition of *Pembrick's Creaturepedia*, designing characters, props, and backgrounds for animated shorts like *The Wingfeather Saga* short film and *Good Boy Richard*, as well as creating art and album covers for a variety of bands, including The Gray Havens. He has a fondness for Swedish fairytales and all magical forests, both of which have been surprisingly vital to his personal artistic growth.

Copyright © 2021 by Wolfbane Books

Published by
Wolfbane Books
1164 Porcher's Bluff Road
Mount Pleasant, SC 29466
www.wolfbanebooks.com

Cover and interior illustrations by Aedan Peterson
Cover and interior design by Brannon McAllister

Hardcover edition ISBN: 978-1-7366106-0-2
First Edition

Printed in the United States of America
10 9 8 7 6 5 4 3 2 1

To my wonderful wife, Rebecca, and my dear daughters, Eisley and Lyla.

Come and see what God has done: he is awesome in his
deeds toward the children of man. (Psalm 66:5)
—KENNETH

To Catherine, my bride and mother of eight.

We will not hide them from their children, but tell to the
coming generation the glorious deeds of YHWH, and his
might, and the wonders that he has done. (Psalm 78:4)
—SHAY

To Nat, the love of my life.

The LORD bless you and keep you;
the LORD make his face to shine upon you and be gracious to you;
the LORD lift up his countenance upon you and
give you peace. (Number 6:24-26)
—AEDAN

Most great stories start a long, long time ago, but this one is so old that no one knows when it began.

Most great stories also happen somewhere far, far away, but this one happens right where you're sitting.

It happens at the dinner table,
    and at your favorite park,
at your bedside in the morning light,
    and even in the dark!
It happens each and every moment,
    every hour, and everywhere!
Because God, who has always been,
    is always there!

That's what this story is about.

We'll jump in somewhere along the way when God made the most beautiful garden!

It was filled with life and light. As the cool wind swirled through the brush and trees, the greenest greens danced around four glistening streams. The fish, the flowers, the flocks, and the fruit were sprinkled with colors of every hue. God's good garden was made for one reason:

So He could dwell with us,
*   and we with Him.*
Always and forever,
*   world without end.*

But you'll never guess what happened next!

God's people chose darkness over light, death over life.
What were they thinking?! They wouldn't listen to the
One who loved them most. So with a broken heart, God
sent them out of the garden. They wandered east and
down to a dark place filled with dust, danger, and death.

They thought they could live without God,
  and surely they tried.
They built a tower for themselves,
  a hollow mountain of pride!

But God wouldn't have it. Every move He
was about to make would be for one reason:

So He could dwell with us,
  and we with Him.
Always and forever,
  world without end.

God put an end to their prideful project. He scattered all the families of the earth across the land to the North, South, East, and West.

It seemed like God was farther away than ever before, but those who knew God knew better.

All creation eagerly waited. A hush fell over God's army of angels. The stars and planets leaned in to listen.

Then it happened…

With the power of a thousand falling mountains, God's voice echoed over the face of the land, and on and on, into forever!

He spoke fresh, love-filled promises to a man called Abraham.

Through one of Abraham's royal sons, God promised to draw all the scattered families of the earth together again.

He promised Abraham a new land filled and flowing with life and light.

Children, grandchildren, great-grandchildren, and great-great-grandchildren would fill the earth like the sand of the seashore and the stars of the sky.

This time, God himself would see it through — and you know why...

So He could dwell with us,
  and we with Him.
Always and forever,
  world without end.

After hundreds of years, with various twists and turns,
God prepared Abraham's family to enter into that lush
garden-land. They were a big, BIG family now, and He
met them at His mountain in the dry dusty desert.

He had them set up a special tent filled and flowing
with all the same wonderful sights and smells of His
mountaintop garden!

He told them to set it up
  in the middle of their camp,
where His presence would shine
  like a big burning lamp!

He arranged it all, just for this reason:

So He could dwell with us,
  and we with Him.
Always and forever,
  world without end.

God led the camp from place to place, until they finally settled in that long-promised land. Then one day, a royal son of Abraham named David ascended the throne. And, like a heavy rain on thirsty land, God showered loving and life-giving promises over him saying, "David's kingdom will never ever end! He shall have a Son who will reign and rule over all the families of the earth, from everlasting to everlasting!"

From the love that God poured out on David there sprang forth the most magnificent garden-palace anyone had ever seen!

Decorated with glittering gold-gilded trees,
fancy-carved fruit, flocks, and flowers flowing in the breeze.

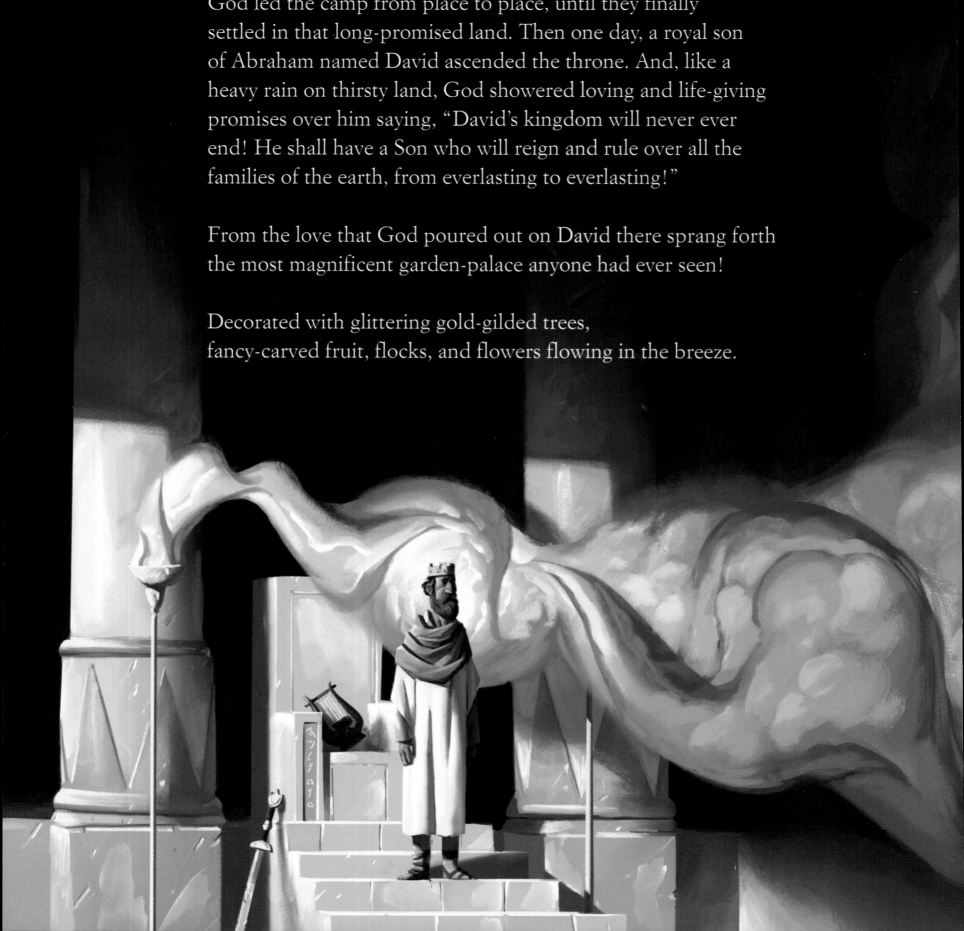

Then when it was all ready, God filled it with His life and light, and a city blossomed around it!

Just like the special tent and the ancient garden long before it, God's temple was built…

So He could dwell with us,
  and we with Him.
Always and forever,
  world without end.

But you'll never guess what happened next!

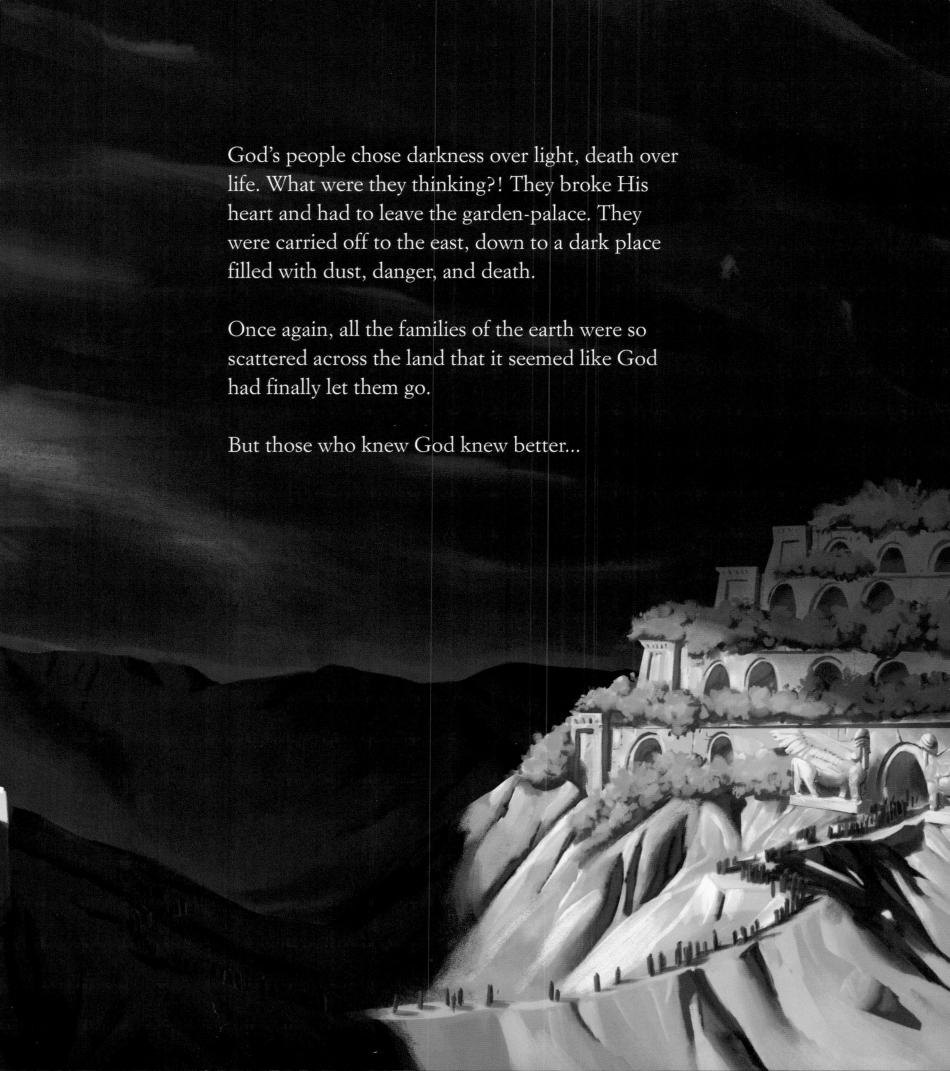

God's people chose darkness over light, death over life. What were they thinking?! They broke His heart and had to leave the garden-palace. They were carried off to the east, down to a dark place filled with dust, danger, and death.

Once again, all the families of the earth were so scattered across the land that it seemed like God had finally let them go.

But those who knew God knew better...

A hush fell over God's heavenly host. The hearts of every bird, beast, and being with breath in its body skipped a beat.

The stars and planets bowed down in the clear silent night.

And with the gentleness of a snowflake landing just before an avalanche, the long-awaited royal Son of David, the Greatest-Great-Grandson of Abraham, the everlasting King, Jesus, Immanuel, God with Us, finally appeared!

He came into the world as light...

To face the darkness on His own.

Defeating death, He filled the whole world with life.

And rose to His royal throne.

In those days, King Jesus poured out
loving and life-filled promises, saying,

"I will always be with you
  and never ever leave you!"
So on and on through the generations,
  His word remains true.

Through the Spirit of this royal Son, all the scattered families of the earth are being drawn back together into God's presence again.

But, you'll never guess what happens next—maybe sooner than you think…

Children, grandchildren, great-grandchildren, and great-great-grandchildren will fill the earth like the sand of the seashore and the stars of the sky.

God will make the whole world into a new land, filled and flowing with His life and light! A city will blossom around His presence—The most magnificent Garden-city anyone will ever see! It's the way God always promised it would be:

So He can dwell with us,
* and we with Him.*
Always and forever,
* world without end.*

As you can see, this is quite a different type of story, because this one is still unfolding!

And you, dear child of God, are actually living right smack in the middle of His great story! These are the days of King Jesus, when all the families of the earth are being drawn back together again. Right now you're living in the land that God will one day turn into the Garden-city!

So keep watch—He's with us! Listen for His voice.

It may come with the power of a thousand falling mountains,
    or like cool rain on dry ground.
It may come with the gentleness of a snowflake landing,
    or without even the slightest sound.

But, know that—
He is dwelling with us
    and we with Him.
Always and forever,
    world without end!

BIBLE REFERENCE GUIDE

The Garden of Eden: *Genesis 2:4-24*

The Fall of Adam & Eve to the Tower of Babel: *Genesis 3-11*

The Great Scattering from Babel: *Genesis 11:8-9*

The Promises to Abraham: *Genesis 12:1-3, 22:17-18*

The Tabernacle: *Exodus 29:45-46, 40:38 & Leviticus 26:9-11*

The Promise to David & A Vision of the Temple: *2 Samuel 7 & 1 Kings 8*

Exile to Babylon: *Isaiah 1:2-7 & 2 Kings 25:8-11*

Immanuel/Nativity: *Matthew 1:18-25 & Luke 1-2*

Jesus as the Light: *John 1:1-14, 8:12*

Jesus Faces Darkness: *Mark 15:33-39 & John 19:16-18 & Colossians 1:9-23*

Jesus Defeats Death: *1 Corinthians 15:20-26, 55-57*

Jesus Ascends to His Throne: *Acts 1:6-11 & 2:29-36 & Ephesians 1:15-22*

King Jesus' Final Command & Pentecost: *Matthew 28:18-20 & Acts 2:1-11*

The Holy City: *Revelation 21:1-4*